BIRDING
Is My Favorite
Video Game

BIRDING
Is My Favorite Video Game

Cartoons about the Natural World
from Bird and Moon

Rosemary Mosco

Andrews McMeel
PUBLISHING®

Andrews McMeel Publishing
a division of Andrews McMeel Universal
1130 Walnut Street, Kansas City, Missouri 64106

www.andrewsmcmeel.com

18 19 20 21 22 SDB 10 9 8 7 6 5 4 3 2 1

ISBN: 978-1-4494-8912-0

Library of Congress Control Number: 2017955394

Editor: Allison Adler
Creative Director: Tim Lynch
Production Editor: Dave Shaw
Production Manager: Chuck Harper

ATTENTION: SCHOOLS AND BUSINESSES

Andrews McMeel books are available at quantity discounts with bulk purchase for educational,
business, or sales promotional use. For information, please e-mail the Andrews McMeel Publishing
Special Sales Department: specialsales@amuniversal.com.

Contents

RARR

AHEM.

Foreword

My first exposure to Rosemary Mosco's work came from the original "Bird and Moon" comic posted on a website of the same name. The sweet nature of the story and the powerful iconography of the art was a delight, and I resolved to keep a close eye on her work in the future.

Since then, Rosemary has evolved into a truly remarkable nature cartoonist. She tackles everything from the silly (newt reproduction!) to the scary (ocean acidification!) with a mixture of humor, hope, and deep knowledge of her subject matter. Her comics are gentle but powerful, clever and enlightening, beautiful and insightful. She has an incredible knack for finding the cuteness in even the ugliest critters, and for presenting complex topics in an easy to understand manner—without compromising the facts. I've never met anyone else who cares so deeply and passionately for the world we live in, and that care is reflected in her work.

When I eventually had the privilege to meet Rosemary in person, I did what any reasonable person would do and asked her to draw some birds to get tattooed onto my flesh. She did so, and I got them—three lovely little cartoon birds on my left arm. I'm privileged to carry her art on my skin, but I'm more privileged to call her a friend. I hope these comics bring you as much delight as they have brought me over the years.

Jeph Jacques
www.questionablecontent.net

My majesty is
simply off the charts.

Part One:
Feathers

If You Find A Baby Songbird Out Of The Nest

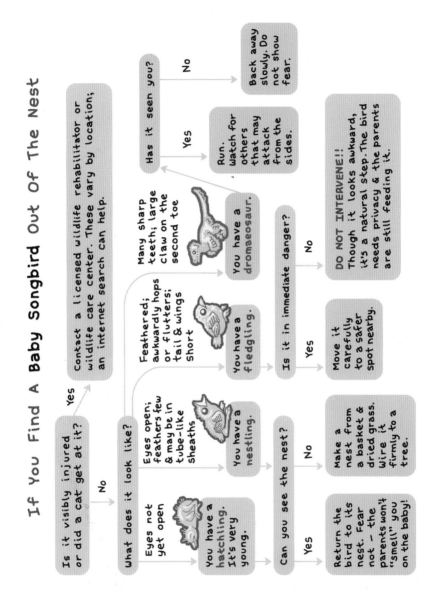

Is it visibly injured or did a cat get at it?

- **Yes** → Contact a licensed wildlife rehabilitator or wildlife care center. These vary by location; an internet search can help.

- **No** →

What does it look like?

- Eyes not yet open → **You have a hatchling. It's very young.**

  Can you see the nest?
  - **Yes** → Return the bird to its nest. Fear not — the parents won't "smell" you on the baby!
  - **No** → Make a nest from a basket & dried grass. Wire it firmly to a tree.

- Eyes open; feathers few & may be in tube-like sheaths → **You have a nestling.**

- Feathered; awkwardly hops or flutters; tail & wings short → **You have a fledgling.**

  Is it in immediate danger?
  - **Yes** → Move it carefully to a safer spot nearby.
  - **No** → DO NOT INTERVENE!! Though it looks awkward, it's a natural step. The bird needs privacy & the parents are still feeding it.

- Many sharp teeth; large claw on the second toe → **You have a dromaeosaur.**

  Has it seen you?
  - **Yes** → Run. Watch for others that may attack from the sides.
  - **No** → Back away slowly. Do not show fear.

Golden-crowned Sparrow

Acorn Woodpecker

Brown Creeper

MacGillivray's Warbler

Common Yellowthroat

California Quail

Vesper Sparrow

Red-breasted Nuthatch

Yellow-headed Blackbird

Mountain Chickadee

Olive-sided Flycatcher

Burrowing Owl

Bird Sound Mnemonics
Songs and Calls of Western North American Birds

Bird Sound Mnemonics
Songs and Calls of Eastern North American Birds

crush

#@!&$%! Empidonax

13

evolution sucks

62 million years ago

50 million years ago

40 million years ago

30 million years ago

20 million years ago

10 million years ago

5 million years ago

present day

14

Foraging Patterns

Brown Creeper

White-breasted
Nuthatch

Yellow-bellied
Sapsucker

. . .

mockingbird problem

Parts of the Bird

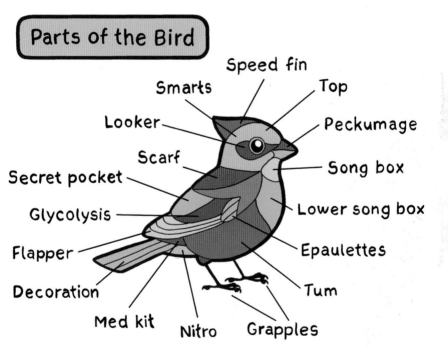

Speed fin

Smarts

Top

Looker

Peckumage

Scarf

Song box

Secret pocket

Glycolysis

Lower song box

Flapper

Epaulettes

Decoration

Tum

Med kit

Nitro

Grapples

Ruffed Grouse Love

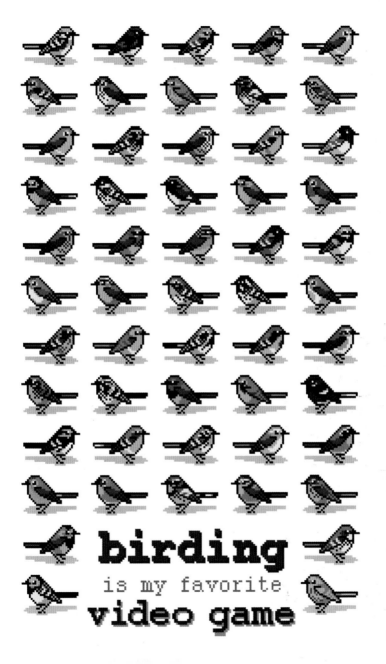

birding *is my favorite* video game

Part Two:
Scales, Fins & Others

the ant and the grasshopper

You lazy grasshopper! Why aren't you collecting food? Don't you know that winter's coming?

I sure do! Only the eggs of my species survive the winter, so I spent this summer laying them by the hundreds. My glorious progeny are poised to emerge at the first sign of spring. Emerge and FEED.

What you should really be asking me is, where the heck did I get this tiny violin?

Bee Club

False Eye Spots
A USEFUL ADAPTATION

Oh man, I had the CRAZIEST dream last night! I was in the meadow, except it wasn't really the <u>same</u> meadow, you know, and suddenly there were all these bad guys! And you and I were fighting them using these swords made of flowers. And then suddenly I realized I wasn't wearing any <u>clothes</u>-

Uh huh. Wow. Great.

small

I.D.

Interrupted Fern

That it's difficult, stuffy, and full of monotony.

And if you disagree, please return your O2.

Some people say that they don't like botany

But plants are amazing, & valuable, too.

versus

Secret Origins of North American Weeds (& critters)

Many common plants and animals in North America weren't found here until a few centuries ago.

Common Reed

- One subspecies is originally from Europe and Asia, where it was used in thatched roofs

- Carried here in the 1800s

- Invades marshes & pushes aside native plants

Yellow Flag Iris

- Brought from Europe in the 1800s

- Spread easily into the Northeast wilderness, altering water flow

House Sparrow

- Imported from Europe (like the Starling & Pigeon)

White Clover

- Brought from Europe in the 1700s

- Used for grazing

Oxeye Daisy

- Native to Europe and Asia

- Arrived in the 1700s

- May have hitched a ride in animal feed

Earthworm

- Wherever glaciers covered the land during the last ice age, earthworms disappeared

- Today's earthworms in the Northeast and Midwest all come from imported stock

Broadleaf Plantain

-Another European plant that spread easily into the cities of the New World

Things I've Learned from Snakes

- color coordination

- camouflage

- bluffing

  RATTLE
  RATTLE

  RAR
  GRR
  BLARR

- behavioral thermoregulation

oh snap

SALAMANDERS need your help

S.O.S.

Salamanders can be shy and secretive...

shhh

...but they're a very important part of the environment.

In some forests, there are more salamanders than any other critter with a backbone.

snort

Also, they're very pretty.

But lately, a new fungal disease is spreading from Asia, probably via the international pet trade.

Called Bsal, it has already wiped out Fire Salamander populations in northern Europe.

But that's only the beginning.

In lab tests on European and North American salamanders, the disease was 100% lethal in 11 of 17 species. (Martel et al., 2014. *Science* 346, 630-631)

It's time to stop Bsal before it spreads everywhere. Here's how to help.

Write to your representatives. Urge them to support legislation that stops the spread of wildlife diseases.

Make life easier for salamanders by supporting the preservation of their habitats.

Argh. Got slime on my screen again.

Don't dump pet salamanders or their water outdoors.

Buy captive-bred, disease-tested pets.

Your slimy neighbors thank you!

secrete weapon

toxic

Part Three:
Seasons

easter bunny

easter horn shark

easter salamander

easter cuttlefish

easter pine snake

Christmas Field Guide

Mistletoe

Highly poisonous semi-parasite of the order Santalales. Its name means "poop twig" and it enjoys watching you kiss.

Reindeer

(a.k.a. Caribou)

Both sexes have antlers. Some sub-species are highly endangered. Questionably aerodynamic.

Poinsettia

A Mexican & Central American plant that looks extra-festive thanks to a bacterial infection.

Holly

Varied plants of the genus *Ilex*. Typically only female holly plants bear red fruit, and only if a male is within an unchaste 25 foot radius.

Two Turtle Doves

Streptopelia turtur & relatives. Increasingly rare. Awkward, noisy, & full of love, much like Christmas.

Partridge in a Pear Tree

Can - can somebody get me down? I'm a ground bird. Please? Somebody? Hello?

★ Happy holidays to those of you who overwinter as adults! ★

Amazing Fall Migrations

Spectacular Songbird Migration

Dazzling Insect Migration

Majestic Hawk Migration

Glorious Garden Snail Migration

Party Animals

PREPARING FOR WINTER
Choose Your Strategy

Get a new coat

Flee south by night

Stockpile food

Temporarily suspend development

HEY SANTA: PLEASE CONSIDER THESE
~ Reindeer Alternatives ~

Humpback Anglerfish
PRO: Very shiny nose
CON: Can't fly

Peregrine Falcon
PRO: Extremely fast
CON: Not a team player

Flying Squid
PRO: Jet-propelled
CON: Can only fly
     for 30 meters

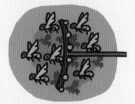

Honeybee Swarm
PRO: Team players
CON: Will stop flying
     if a suitable nest
     cavity is found

Quetzalcoatlus
CON: Extinct
PRO: You only need to clone one

Happy Halloween! Be sure to wear bright colors to deter predators.

Part Four:
So You Want to
Be a Biologist

biologist
vacation photos

This is my favorite photo from the trip. It's a Spinulose Wood-Fern! See how the first lowest pinnule is longer than the adjacent pinnules?

Gotcha.

Oh man - and this is a great one. It's the less common "alba" form of the female Orange Sulphur butterfly!

And if you stare long enough at this photo of Ring-Billed Gulls, you'll notice that one of them is really a Glaucous Gull!

Uh huh...

Did you get any pictures of the actual wedding?

Well, I *think* you can see the bride and groom in the background of this awesome shot of owl pellets.

Make sure you send them extra copies.

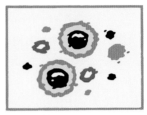

Eyespots (to confuse my enemies)

Display Crest

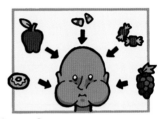

Cheek Pouches (to store snacks)

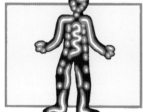

Bioluminescent Photophores

Photosynthetic Organ That Produces
a Constant Supply of Sugar

All the Parts of the
Tarantula Hawk Wasp

Attenborough

urban biology
BINGO

Black Locust Tree	House Sparrow (female)	Red-legged Grasshopper	Bumblebee (any species)	Red-tailed Hawk
Mallard Duck (male)	Rock Pigeon (red morph)	White-tailed Deer	Cabbage White	Northern Mockingbird
Rock Pigeon (pied morph)	House Sparrow (male)	Free Space	Mallard Duck (female)	Red Clover
European Starling	Painted Turtle (or any turtle)	American Robin	Box Elder Tree (a.k.a. Ash-leaved Maple)	Rock Pigeon (red bar morph)
Eastern Cottontail (or any rabbit)	Chicory	Eastern Gray Squirrel (or any squirrel)	Canada Goose	Milky Slug

urban biology
BINGO

American Robin	Little Brown Bat (or any bat)	Canada Goose	Painted Turtle (or any turtle)	House Sparrow (male)
Raccoon	White-tailed Deer	Mallard Duck (male)	Rock Pigeon (spread morph)	Black Locust Tree
Chimney Swift (or any swift)	Rock Pigeon (red morph)	Free Space	Red-legged Grasshopper	Red-tailed Hawk
House Sparrow (female)	Northern Mockingbird	American Bullfrog	Eastern Gray Squirrel (or any squirrel)	Milky Slug
White Clover	Mallard Duck (female)	Bumblebee (any species)	Cabbage White	Rock Pigeon (showing off)

Feeling lonely?

Just remember,
you're not alone.

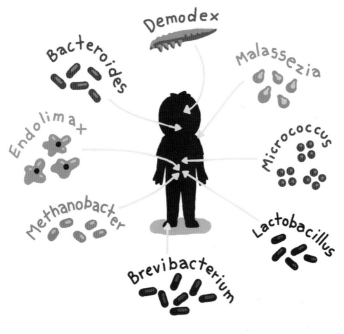

YOU ARE NEVER ALONE.

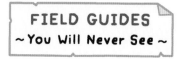

FIELD GUIDES
~ You Will Never See ~

MOSSES
THROUGH
BINOCULARS

HAWKS
FROM
ABOVE

TREES
OF
ANTARCTICA
? ? ?

BIRDS
FROM THAT
ONE DREAM
I HAD

BORING
LEAVES

WHALES
from
INSIDE

HOUSE~
PLANTS
From
OUTSIDE

FIELD GUIDES
of
NORTH
AMERICA

science + art = ♥

This Year's Top Ten Posts

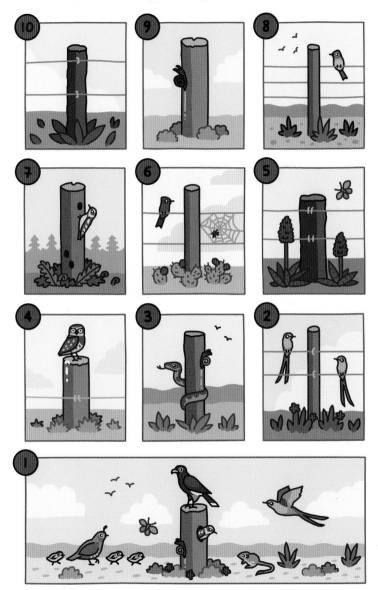

♥ Animal Dating Profiles ♥

♥ Digger_Wasp_2014

Status: Single

About Me: No more games! I've had my heart broken too many times. I just want to meet a nice lady who is not an orchid.

♥ Gulper Eel 42

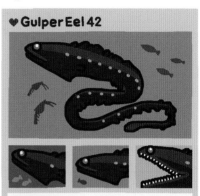

Status: Single

About Me: I may seem shy at first, but once you get to know me I really open up :D

♥ Smalltooth_Sawfish_XOXO

Status: Single, Critically endangered

About Me: I'm having trouble finding a partner, and I'm so tired of hearing my friends say that there are plenty of fish in the sea. Drop me a line!

♥ ~Sanderling~

Status: Single

About Me: I like long walks up the beach and down the beach and up the beach and down the beach and up the beach and down the beach and

When I Grow Up...

Common Five-lined Skink

Luna Moth

Spotted Salamander

American Robin

Common Green Darner

Black Swallowtail

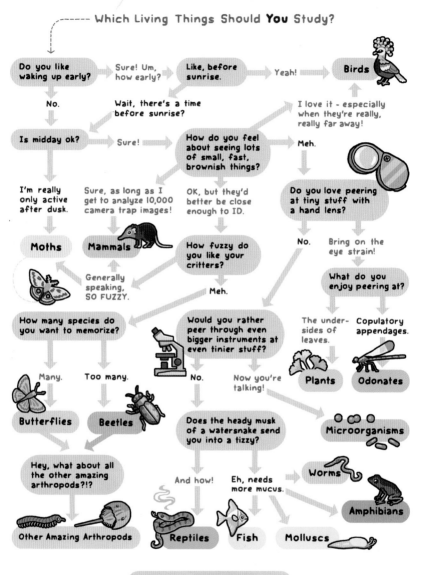

Which Living Things Should **You** Study?

Do you like waking up early? → Sure! Um, how early? → **Like, before sunrise.** → Yeah! → **Birds**

No. ↓

Wait, there's a time before sunrise?

Is midday ok? → Sure! → **How do you feel about seeing lots of small, fast, brownish things?**

I love it - especially when they're really, really far away! ↑ → **Birds**

Meh. ↓

I'm really only active after dusk. ↓ **Moths**

Sure, as long as I get to analyze 10,000 camera trap images! ↓ **Mammals**

OK, but they'd better be close enough to ID. ↓

Do you love peering at tiny stuff with a hand lens?

No. Bring on the eye strain!

What do you enjoy peering at?

How fuzzy do you like your critters?

Generally speaking, SO FUZZY. → **Moths**

Meh. ↓

How many species do you want to memorize?

Would you rather peer through even bigger instruments at even tinier stuff?

The undersides of leaves. **Plants**

Copulatory appendages. **Odonates**

Many. **Butterflies**

Too many. **Beetles**

No. ↓

Now you're talking! → **Microorganisms**

Does the heady musk of a watersnake send you into a tizzy?

Hey, what about all the other amazing arthropods?!? ↓ **Other Amazing Arthropods**

And how! → **Reptiles**

Eh, needs more mucus. → **Fish**

→ **Worms**

→ **Molluscs**

→ **Amphibians**

I don't have to follow your rules! ↓ **Fungi**

A Few Women Naturalists to Know

"Of what matter is a little water in one's boots, when seeking the Gardens of the Gods?"
-Grace Greylock Niles, 1904

"Looking around us we mark the endless variety of graceful forms in tree and leaf and flower. The earth is teeming with luxuriance..."
-Catharine Parr Traill, 1894

TROMP
TROMP

"Never be content with the common name only. Search, inquire, study, until you have discovered the title by which science recognizes your favorite."
-Annie Sawyer Downs, 1892

"Provided with glass and note-book and dressed in inconspicuous colors, proceed to some good birdy place...to look and listen in silence."
-Florence Merriam Bailey, 1902

"I have wandered alone for the most part...Called 'crazy,' a 'fool'...The flowers being my only society and the manuals the only literature for months together. Happy, happy hours!"
-Kate Furbish, 1908

Definitely a fashion "do."

Part Five:
Tips & Tricks

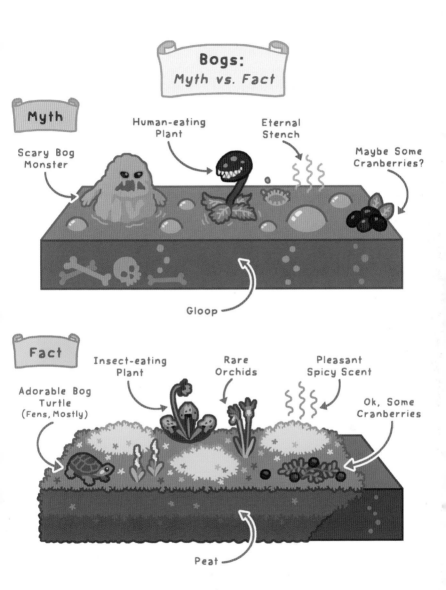

Bogs:
Myth vs. Fact

Myth

Scary Bog Monster

Human-eating Plant

Eternal Stench

Maybe Some Cranberries?

Gloop

Fact

Adorable Bog Turtle (Fens, Mostly)

Insect-eating Plant

Rare Orchids

Pleasant Spicy Scent

Ok, Some Cranberries

Peat

Animal Cheat Sheet*
How to spot the difference!

Dolphin vs Porpoise

Oceanic dolphins are often slimmer, with a curvier dorsal fin and longer beak – but there are many exceptions & many kinds of dolphin.

I also have flatter, blunter teeth, but that's hard to see from a boat.

Luckily, there are only 6 species in the porpoise family, so why not just get to know 'em? They're cute and some are very endangered!

Lizard vs Salamander

Salamanders are amphibians (like frogs).
Lizards are reptiles (like turtles).

Some differences: salamanders have no scales or claws, and often have wet skin.

Moth vs Butterfly

Caution: some moths are colorful, and some butterflies are not!

One tip: in most (but not all) cases, their antennae are differently shaped.

club tip

Cat Footprint vs Dog Footprint

One difference: cat prints make a "c" shape for cat. Dog prints make an "x" for X-TREEM.

Pigeon vs Dove

They're in the same family, and people use the terms kinda arbitrarily.

Coo!

Usually, we call the smaller birds "doves," but not always!

Coo!

Inchworm vs Earthworm

I'm an insect, and one day I'll turn into a beautiful geometer moth!

Luckily, I will always be a gorgeous earthworm.

* Recommended as a rough guide only. Common names are messy. Not to be used in place of a biology course or in the event of an actual moth attack.

the climate change shuffle

Nature is a complex dance.

But as the climate changes rapidly, many critters are changing their moves to try and keep up.

Some are heading north.

Mountain creatures are climbing to escape the heat.

Different parts of the climate affect creatures differently...

...causing conflicts...

HAHA Yummm

eep!

...and altering relationships.

And you thought your high school prom was messy.

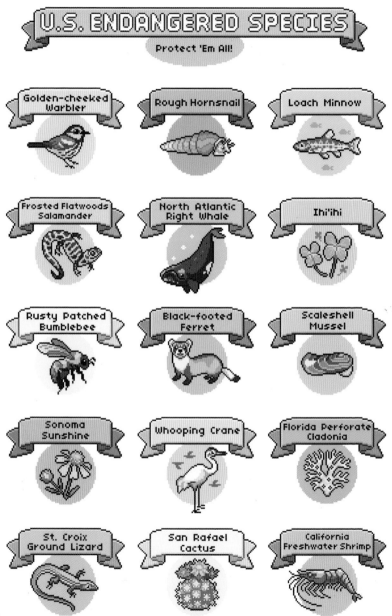

U.S. ENDANGERED SPECIES

Protect 'Em All!

Golden-cheeked Warbler

Rough Hornsnail

Loach Minnow

Frosted Flatwoods Salamander

North Atlantic Right Whale

Ihi'ihi

Rusty Patched Bumblebee

Black-footed Ferret

Scaleshell Mussel

Sonoma Sunshine

Whooping Crane

Florida Perforate Cladonia

St. Croix Ground Lizard

San Rafael Cactus

California Freshwater Shrimp

Fashion Tips
from nature

Poisonous? Share the news with bold stripes.

Or coordinate with a toxic friend!

Keep your dates on their toes with these terrifying eyespots.

These classic looks are timeless and practical.

Leaf

Bark

Bird Poop

False Head

Inflatable air sacs keep you party-ready.

Amaze your crush with your ability to sport this style yet still move and find food.

Ghosts of the Northeast Woods

Peregrine Falcons were gone from the East by the 1960s. Reintroduced birds are a mix of subspecies.

Woodland Caribou once roamed through several Eastern states and provinces. They're now gone from half their range.

Once the widest-ranging hoofed critter on the continent, Elk disappeared from the area in the 1800s.

Intense hunting efforts and habitat loss pushed the Cougar out of the East by the early 1900s.

Persecution and poaching removed the docile, shy Timber Rattlesnake from much of its range.

The American Chestnut was one of the most common trees. An introduced disease killed almost all adults by 1930.

Why do Hammerhead Sharks have hammer heads?

X Extra space for fancy jewelery

X Lift for brief but exhilarating flights

✓ To spot, pin, and dispatch flappy prey

Hom nom nom nom

SHARK FORT

X A tool for building undersea forts

If climate change were a dude...

...we'd kick him out of the house.

One AW109 Grand Versace
VIP Private Helicopter:

$6.6 million

Saving all the
world's lemurs:

$7.6 million

Both:

wheeeeeeeee

Priceless

Animals with Misleading Names

Electric Eel

Not an eel.

Mountain Goat

Not a goat.

Maned Wolf

Not a wolf.

King Cobra

Not a cobra. Also, snakes are typically self-governing.

Peacock Mantis Shrimp

Not a peacock.
Not a mantis.
Also, not a shrimp.

Horny Toad

Not a toad.
Only thinks of you as a friend.

Mayfly

Active through the spring and summer.

Eastern Kingbird

Found in the West. Many birds do not recognize its authority.

a guide to
Nature Names
FOR YOUR BABY

Good

🌿Violet ✳Lily ☁Summer

🌾Rowan 🌿Ash 🌾Lavender

🌾Heather 🐦Robin 🌞Dawn

Bad

🐦Tawny Frogmouth 🍄Blewit

🍁Virginia Creeper 🌿Cheeseweed

🐑Compressed Flapwort

🐗Screaming Hairy Armadillo

GREAT

🪰Dragonhunter 🌿Centaury

🦅Bat Falcon 🦎Hellbender

🌿Mother of Thousands

archaeopteryx

bifericeras

calymene

doedicurus

edaphosaurus

fukuiraptor

griphognathus

hesperornis

indricotherium

jobaria

kentrosaurus

laggania

megaloceros

nothosaurus

ophthalmosaurus

pteraspis

quetzalcoatlus

raphus

smilodon

telicomys

utahraptor

vauxia

waptia

xenacanthus

yandusaurus

zalambdalestes

know your prehistory.

Some Quotes about Climate Change

"I believe that climate change is fundamentally the greatest threat to the integrity of our national parks that we have ever experienced."
-Jonathan B. Jarvis, Director, U.S. National Park Service

"How could I look my grandchildren in the eye and say I knew about this – and I did nothing?"
– Sir David Attenborough

"It's hard even for people like me to believe, to see that climate change is actually doing what our worst fears dictated. It's starting to give me chills, to tell you the truth."
– Jennifer Francis, Research Professor, Rutgers University

"PEEP PEEP PEEP PEEP PEEP PEEP PEEP PEEP PEEP PEEP PEEP PEEP PEEP PEEP PEEP PEEP PEEP PEEP PEEP PEEP PEEP PEEP PEEP PEEP PEEP PEEP PEEP PEEP PEEP PEEP PEEP PEEP PEEP PEEP PEEP PEEP PEEP PEEP PEEP PEEP PEEP PEEP PEEP PEEP PEEP PEEP PEEP PEEP PEEP PEEP PEEP PEEP PEEP PEEP PEEP PEEP PEEP PEEP PEEP PEEP PEEP PEEP PEEP PEEP PEEP."
– Irate wildlife

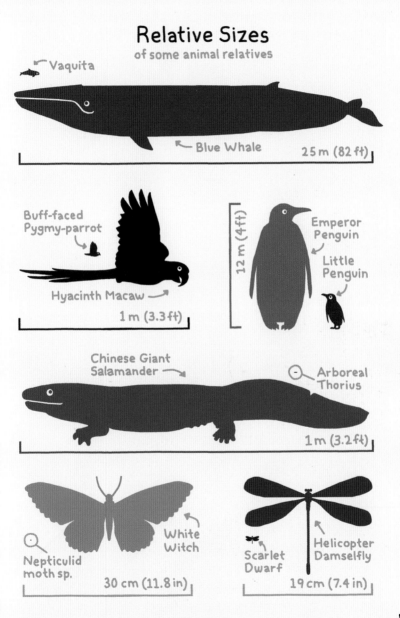

Relative Sizes

of some animal relatives

Vaquita

Blue Whale
25 m (82 ft)

Buff-faced
Pygmy-parrot

Hyacinth Macaw
1 m (3.3 ft)

12 m (4 ft)

Emperor
Penguin

Little
Penguin

Chinese Giant
Salamander

Arboreal
Thorius

1 m (3.2 ft)

White
Witch

Nepticulid
moth sp.
30 cm (11.8 in)

Scarlet
Dwarf

Helicopter
Damselfly

19 cm (7.4 in)

Take action for animals.

Because they are really, really bad at it.

Threat displays of non-threatening animals

Recently molted crayfish

Dry Riesling

Slowly sinking flakes
of oceanic detritus

Fruity Merlot

Raw ostrich egg
smashed with rock

Full-bodied
Pinot Noir

Sugary liquid stored in
gaster and regurgitated
upon request

Sparkling
Dessert Wine

Species Index

Acacia, Whistling Thorn
Acacia drepanolobium
(page 27)

Aracari, Collared
Pteroglossus torquatus
(page 46)

Actinomycetes/Actinobacteria
(page 45)

Archaeopteryx
(page 83)

Agaric, Fly
Amanita muscaria
(page 49)

Attenborough, David
Homo attenboroughensis
(page 55)

Anglerfish, Humpback
Melanocetus johnsonii
(page 48)

Bacteroides
(page 59)

Anole, Green
Anolis carolinensis
(page 88)

Badger, European
Meles meles
(page 46)

Ant
Formicidae
(pages 23, 50)

Bat, Little Brown
Myotis lucifugus
(page 56)

Ant, Honeypot
Myrmecocystus mexicanus
(page 89)

Bear, Asiatic Black
Ursus thibetanus
(page 86)

Aphid, Apple
Aphis pomi
(page 50)

Bear, Polar
Ursus maritimus
(page 86)

Bee, Bumble
Bombus sp.
(page 24)

Blue, Adonis
Polyommatus bellargus
(page 66)

Bee, Carpenter
Xylocopa sp.
(page 24)

Blue, Karner
Lycaeides melissa samuelis
(page 86)

Bee, European Honey
Apis mellifera
(page 48)

Brevibacterium
(page 59)

Bee, Rusty Patched Bumble
Bombus affinis
(page 72)

Brittle Star
Ophionotus victoriae
(page 71)

Bee-eater, European
Merops apiaster
(page 25)

Broadbill, Green
Calyptomena viridis
(page 46)

Bifericeras
(page 83)

Buckeye, Common
Junonia coenia
(page 71)

Bird, Terror
Phorusrhacidae
(page 14)

Budgerigar
Melopsittacus undulatus
(page 49)

Bird-of-paradise, King of
Saxony
Pteridophora alberti
(page 73)

Bullfrog, American
Lithobates catesbeianus
(page 56)

Blackbird, Yellow-headed
Xanthocephalus xanthocephalus
(page 9)

Bunting, Indigo
Passerina cyanea
(page 10)

Bunting, Lazuli
Passerina amoena
(page 71)

Chat, Yellow-breasted
Icteria virens
(page 21)

Bushbaby, Senegal
Galago senegalensis
(page 49)

Chestnut, American
Castanea dentata
(page 74)

Cactus, San Rafael
Pediocactus despainii
(page 72)

Chickadee, Mountain
Poecile gambeli
(page 9)

Calymene
(page 83)

Chickory, Common
Cichorium intybus
(page 56)

Caribou
Rangifer tarandus
(pages 43, 74)

Chipmunk, Alpine
Tamias alpinus
(page 71)

Catbird, Gray
Dumetella carolinensis
(page 10)

Chipmunk, Eastern
Tamias striatus
(page 49)

Caterpillar, Giant Swallowtail
Papilio cresphontes
(page 73)

Chrysobothris azurea
(page 66)

Caterpillar, Linden Looper
Erannis tiliaria
(page 70)

Cladonia, Florida Perforate
Cladonia perforata
(page 72)

Chameleon, Jackson's
Trioceros jacksonii
(page 61)

Clover, Red
Trifolium pratense
(page 56)

Clover, White
Trifolium repens
(pages 32, 56)

Cranberry, Large
Vaccinium macrocarpon
(page 69)

Clownfish, Orange
Amphiprion percula
(page 82)

Crane, Whooping
Grus americana
(pages 72, 86)

Cobra, King
Ophiophagus hannah
(page 80)

Creeper, Brown
Certhia americana
(page 9, 15)

Copperhead
Agkistrodon contortrix
(page 40)

Crematogaster mimosae
(page 27)

Cornsnake, Red
Pantherophis guttatus
(pages 63, 88)

Crow, American
Corvus brachyrhynchos
(page 19)

Cottontail, Eastern
Sylvilagus floridanus
(page 56)

Cuckoo, Common
Cuculus canorus
(page 71)

Cougar
Puma concolor
(page 74)

Cuttlefish, Common
Sepia officinalis
(page 42)

Crab, Atlantic Horseshoe
Limulus polyphemus
(page 66)

Daisy, Oxeye
Leucanthemum vulgare
(page 32)

Crab, King
Neolithodes yaldwyni
(page 71)

Damselfly, Helicopter
Megaloprepus caerulatus
(page 85)

Darner, Common Green
Anax junius
(pages 44, 65)

Dromaeosaur
Dromaeosauridae
(page 8)

Deer, White-tailed
Odocoileus virginianus
(page 56)

Duskywing
Either *Erynnis juvenalis* or
Erynnis horatius
(page 28)

Demodex
(page 59)

Dwarf, Scarlet
Nannophya pygmaea
(page 85)

Doedicurus
(page 83)

Earthworm, Common
Lumbricus terrestris
(pages 32, 66)

Dolphin, Atlantic
White-sided
Lagenorhynchus acutus
(page 70)

Edaphosaurus
(page 83)

Dolphin, South Asian River
Platanista gangetica
(page 78)

Eel, Electric
Electrophorus electricus
(page 80)

Dodo
Raphus cucullatus
(page 83)

Eel, Gulper
Eurypharynx pelecanoides
(page 64)

Dove, European Turtle
Streptopelia turtur
(pages 43, 70)

Elfin, Brown
Callophrys augustinus
(page 70)

Dragonfish, Little
Eurypegasus draconis
(page 61)

Elk
Cervus canadensis
(page 74)

Elk, Irish
Megaloceros giganteus
(page 83)

Fern, Spinulose Wood
Dryopteris carthusiana
(page 53)

Empid
Empidonax sp.
(page 13)

Fern, Walking
Asplenium rhizophyllum
(page 50)

Endolimax
(page 59)

Ferret, Black-footed
Mustela nigripes
(page 72)

Falcon, Peregrine
Falco peregrinus
(pages 48, 74)

Fly, Greater Bee
Bombylius major
(page 25)

Fern, Bracken
Pteridium aquilinum
(page 49)

Fly, Robber
Laphria sp.
(page 25)

Fern, Christmas
Polystichum acrostichoides
(page 50)

Flycatcher, Olive-sided
Contopus cooperi
(page 9)

Fern, Hart's Tongue
Asplenium scolopendrium
(page 50)

Flycatcher, Scissor-tailed
Tyrannus forficatus
(page 63)

Fern, Interrupted
Osmunda claytoniana
(page 29)

Flycatcher, Vermilion
Pyrocephalus rubinus
(page 63)

Fern, Sensitive
Onoclea sensibilis
(page 50)

Frog, Panamanian Golden
Atelopus zeteki
(page 55)

Frog, Strawberry Poison Dart
Oophaga pumilio
(page 66)

 Greensnake, Smooth
Opheodrys vernalis
(page 33)

 Frog, Wallace's Flying
Rhacophorus nigropalmatus
(page 61)

 Griphognathus
(page 83)

 Fukuiraptor
(page 83)

 Grouse, Ruffed
Bonasa umbellus
(page 20)

 Ginkgo
Ginkgo biloba
(page 66)

 Gull, Glaucous
Larus hyperboreus
(page 53)

 Giraffe
Giraffa camelopardalis
(page 27)

 Hairstreak, Gray
Strymon melinus
(page 73)

 Goat, Mountain
Oreamnos americanus
(page 80)

 Hammerhead, Greater
Sphyrna mokarran
(page 75)

 Goose, Canada
Branta canadensis
(page 56)

 Hare, Snowshoe
Lepus americanus
(page 47)

 Grasshopper
Caelifera
(page 23)

 Hawk, Broad-winged
Buteo platypterus
(page 44)

Grasshopper, Red-legged
Melanoplus femurrubrum
(page 56)

 Hawk, Harris's
Parabuteo unicinctus
(page 63)

Hawk, Red-tailed
Buteo jamaicensis
(pages 19, 44, 56)

Ihi'ihi
Marsilea villosa
(page 72)

Hawk, Sharp-shinned
Accipiter striatus
(page 44)

Indri
Indri indri
(page 79)

Hellbender
Cryptobranchus alleganiensis
(page 37)

Indricotherium
(aka *Paraceratherium*)
(page 83)

Hesperornis
(page 83)

Iris, Yellow Flag
Iris pseudacorus
(page 32)

Holly, American
Ilex opaca
(page 43)

Jay, Blue
Cyanocitta cristata
(page 19)

Hurdia victoria
(page 51)

Jewelwing, Superb
Calopteryx amata
(page 66)

Hornsnail, Rough
Pleurocera foremani
(page 72)

Jobaria
(page 83)

Hummingbird, Ruby-throated
Archilochus colubris
(page 49)

Kangaroo Rat, Desert
Dipodomys deserti
(page 63)

Iguana, Fiji Banded
Brachylophus fasciatus
(page 86)

Katydid, Leaf
Mimetica sp.
(page 73)

Keelback, Tiger
Rhabdophis tigrinus
(page 40)

Lizard, Frill-necked
Chlamydosaurus kingii
(page 61)

Kentrosaurus
(page 83)

Lizard, Greater Earless
Cophosaurus texanus
(page 70)

Kingbird, Eastern
Tyrannus tyrannus
(pages 19, 80)

Lizard, Philippine Sailfin
Hydrosaurus pustulatus
(page 61)

Kingsnake, Gray-banded
Lampropeltis alterna
(page 33)

Lizard, St. Croix Ground
Ameiva polops
(page 72)

Lactobacillus
(page 59)

Lizard, Sulawesi Gliding
Draco spilonotus
(page 61)

Laggania
(page 83)

Lizard, Texas Horned
Phrynosoma cornutum
(page 80)

Lemur, Brown Mouse
Microcebus rufus
(page 79)

Locust, Black
Robinia pseudoacacia
(page 56)

Lemur, Red-ruffed
Varecia rubra
(page 79)

Lousewort, Furbish's
Pedicularis furbishiae
(page 67)

Lemur, Ring-tailed
Lemur catta
(page 79)

Lyrebird, Superb
Menura novaehollandiae
(page 55)

Macaw, Hyacinth
Anodorhynchus hyacinthinus
(page 85)

Micrococcus
(page 59)

Macaw, Spix's
Cyanopsitta spixii
(page 86)

Milkweed, Common
Asclepias syriaca
(page 31)

Maidenhair, Northern
Adiantum pedatum
(page 50)

Millipede, Striped
Ommatoiulus sabulosus
(page 66)

Malassezia
(page 59)

Minnow, Loach
Rhinichthys cobitis
(page 72)

Mallard
Anas platyrhynchos
(page 56)

Mistletoe, European
Viscum album
(page 43)

Maple, Boxelder
Acer negundo
(page 56)

Mockingbird, Northern
Mimus polyglottos
(pages 16, 56)

Mayfly
Ephemeroptera
(page 80)

Monarch
Danaus plexippus
(pages 31, 44, 73)

Meerkat
Suricata suricatta
(page 55)

Moony, Silver
Monodactylus argenteus
(page 66)

Methanobacter
(page 59)

Moth, Io
Automeris io
(pages 66, 88)

Moth, Luna
Actias luna
(page 65)

Newt, Great Crested
Triturus cristatus
(page 61)

Moth, Morgan's Spinx
Xanthopan morganii
(page 49)

Nothosaurus
(page 83)

Moth, Rosy Maple
Dryocampa rubicunda
(page 70)

Nuthatch, Red-breasted
Sitta canadensis
(page 9)

Moth, Snowberry Clearwing
Hemaris diffinis
(page 25)

Nuthatch, White-breasted
Sitta carolinensis
(page 15)

Mourning Cloak
Nymphalis antiopa
(page 47)

Oarfish, Giant
Regalecus glesne
(page 61)

Mussel, Scaleshell
Leptodea leptodon
(page 72)

Ophthalmosaurus
(page 83)

Nepticulidae
(page 85)

Orchid, Common Spotted
Dactylorhiza fuchsii
(page 63)

Newt, Chinese Fire Belly
Cynops orientalis
(page 37)

Orchid, Dragon's Mouth
Arethusa bulbosa
(page 69)

Newt, Eastern
Notophthalmus viridescens
(pages 34, 37)

Orchid, Fly
Ophyrs insectifera
(page 64)

Ovenbird
Seiurus aurocapilla
(pages 10, 21)

Penguin, Emperor
Aptenodytes forsteri
(page 85)

Owl, Barred
Strix varia
(page 38)

Penguin, Little
Eudyptula minor
(page 85)

Owl, Burrowing
Athene cunicularia
(pages 9, 63)

Phoebe, Say's
Sayornis saya
(page 63)

Owl, Pale
Caligo telamonius
(pages 26, 73)

Pigeon, Feral Rock
Columba livia
(page 56)

Pangolin, Philippine
Manis culionensis
(page 86)

Pigeon, Victoria Crowned
Goura victoria
(page 66)

Birds

Parrot, Buff-faced Pygmy
Micropsitta pusio
(page 85)

Pigeon, Wood
Columba palumbus
(page 70)

Partridge, Gray
Perdix perdix
(page 43)

Pinesnake, Eastern
Pituophis melanoleucus
(page 42)

Parula, Northern
Setophaga americana
(page 21)

Pitohui, Hooded
Pitohui dichrous
(page 40)

Parula, Tropical
Setophaga pitiayumi
(page 21)

Plant, Purple Pitcher
Sarracenia purpurea
(page 69)

Plantain, Broadleaf
Plantago major
(page 32)

Plover, European Golden
Pluvialis apricaria
(page 84)

Poinsettia
Euphorbia pulcherrima
(page 43)

Porpoise, Harbor
Phocoena phocoena
(page 70)

Potoo, Common
Nyctibius griseus
(page 46)

Prairie-chicken, Greater
Tympanuchus cupido
(page 73)

Pteraspis
(page 83)

Quail, California
Callipepla californica
(pages 9, 63)

Queensnake
Regina septemvittata
(page 89)

Quetzalcoatlus
(pages 48, 83)

Raccoon, North American
Procyon lotor
(page 56)

Racer, North American (baby)
Coluber constrictor
(page 33)

Rattlesnake, Timber
Crotalus horridus
(pages 33, 74)

Redstart, American
Setophaga ruticilla
(page 21)

Redstart, Painted
Myioborus pictus
(page 21)

Reed, Common
Phragmites australis
(page 32)

Robin, American
Turdus migratorius
(pages 56, 65)

Robin, European
Erithacus rubecula
(page 71)

Salamander, Chinese Giant
Andrias davidianus
(page 85)

Seal, Harp
Pagophilus groenlandicus
(page 58)

Salamander, Common Fire
Salamandra salamandra
(page 37)

Sengi, Black and Rufous
Rhynchocyon petersi
(page 66)

Salamander, Frosted Flatwoods
Ambystoma cingulatum
(page 72)

Shark, Horn
Heterodontus francisci
(page 42)

Salamander, Red
Pseudotriton ruber
(page 70)

Shrew, Northern Short-tailed
Blarina brevicauda
(page 40)

Salamander, Spotted
Ambystoma maculatum
(pages 38, 42, 65)

Shrimp, California Freshwater
Syncaris pacifica
(page 72)

Salamander, Yonahlossee
Plethodon yonahlossee
(page 37)

Shrimp, Peacock Mantis
Odontodactylus scyllarus
(page 80)

Sanderling
Calidris alba
(page 64)

Siren, Greater
Siren lacertina
(page 61)

Sapsucker, Yellow-bellied
Sphyrapicus varius
(page 15)

Skink, Common Five-lined
Plestiodon fasciatus
(page 65)

Sawfish, Smalltooth
Pristis pectinata
(page 64)

Slug, California Banana
Ariolimax californicus
(page 66)

Slug, Milky
Deroceras reticulatum
(page 56)

Sphagnum
Sphagnum spp.
(page 69)

Smilodon
(page 83)

Spoonbill, Roseate
Platalea ajaja
(page 51)

Snail, Garden
Cornu aspersum
(page 44)

Squid, Japanese Flying
Todarodes pacificus
(page 48)

Snake, Green Vine
Oxybelis fulgidus
(page 46)

Squid, Vampire
Vampyroteuthis infernalis
(page 89)

Snake, Paradise Flying
Chrysopelea paradisi
(page 61)

Squirrel, Eastern Gray
Sciurus carolinensis
(page 56)

Sparrow, Golden-crowned
Zonotrichia atricapilla
(page 9)

Starling, European
Sturnus vulgaris
(page 56)

Sparrow, House
Passer domesticus
(pages 32, 56)

Stick Insect
Phasmatodea
(page 46)

Sparrow, Vesper
Pooecetes gramineus
(page 9)

Stinkhorn, Lattice
Clathrus ruber
(page 66)

Sparrow, White-throated
Zonotrichia albicollis
(page 10)

Sulphur, Orange
Colias eurytheme
(page 53)

Sunshine, Sonoma
Blennosperma bakeri
(page 72)

Tortoise, Radiated
Astrochelys radiata
(page 86)

Swallowtail, Black
Papilio polyxenes
(page 65)

Toucan, Keel-billed
Ramphastos sulfuratus
(page 49)

Swallowtail, Giant
Papilio cresphontes
(page 71)

Towhee, Eastern
Pipilo erythrophthalmus
(page 10)

Swift, Chimney
Chaetura pelagica
(page 56)

Towhee, Green-tailed
Pipilo chlorurus
(page 71)

Telicomys
(page 83)

Treefrog, Gray
Hyla versicolor
(page 73)

Thorius, Arboreal
Thorius arboreus
(page 85)

Treefrog, Morelet's
Agalychnis moreletii
(page 86)

Thrush, Bicknell's
Catharus bicknelli
(page 58)

Turkey, Wild
Meleagris gallopavo
(page 12)

Thrush, Wood
Hylocichla mustelina
(page 47)

Turtle, Bog
Glyptemys muhlenbergii
(page 69)

Toad, Cane
Rhinella marina
(page 40)

Turtle, Common Snapping
Chelydra serpentina
(page 36)

Turtle, Painted
Chrysemys picta
(page 56)

Vulture, Turkey
Cathartes aura
(page 10)

Turtle, Wood
Glyptemys insculpta
(page 46)

Waptia
(page 83)

Utahraptor
(page 83)

Warbler, Bachman's
Vermivora bachmanii
(page 21)

Vaquita
Phocoena sinus
(page 85)

Warbler, Bay-breasted
Setophaga castanea
(page 21)

Vauxia
(page 83)

Warbler, Black-and-white
Mniotilta varia
(page 21)

Viceroy
Limenitis archippus
(page 73)

Warbler, Blackburnian
Setophaga fusca
(page 21)

Violetear, Mexican
Colibri thalassinus
(page 88)

Warbler, Blackpoll
Setophaga striata
(page 21)

Vireo, Red-eyed
Vireo olivaceus
(page 10)

Warbler, Black-throated Blue
Setophaga caerulescens
(pages 10, 21)

Vulture, Egyptian
Neophron percnopterus
(page 89)

Warbler, Black-throated Gray
Setophaga nigrescens
(page 21)

Warbler, Black-throated Green
Setophaga virens
(pages 10, 21)

 Warbler, Golden-crowned
Basileuterus culicivorus
(page 21)

 Warbler, Blue-winged
Vermivora cyanoptera
(pages 10, 21)

 Warbler, Golden-winged
Vermivora chrysoptera
(page 21)

 Warbler, Canada
Cardellina canadensis
(page 21)

Warbler, Grace's
Setophaga graciae
(page 21)

 Warbler, Cape May
Setophaga tigrina
(page 21)

 Warbler, Hermit
Setophaga occidentalis
(page 21)

Warbler, Cerulean
Setophaga cerulea
(page 21)

 Warbler, Hooded
Setophaga citrina
(page 21)

 Warbler, Chestnut-sided
Setophaga pensylvanica
(pages 10, 21)

Warbler, Kentucky
Geothlypis formosa
(page 21)

 Warbler, Colima
Oreothlypis crissalis
(page 21)

 Warbler, Kirtland's
Setophaga kirtlandii
(page 21)

 Warbler, Connecticut
Oporornis agilis
(page 21)

 Warbler, Lucy's
Oreothlypis luciae
(page 21)

 Warbler, Golden-cheeked
Setophaga chrysoparia
(pages 21, 72)

 Warbler, MacGillivray's
Geothlypis tolmiei
(page 9)

Warbler, Magnolia
Setophaga magnolia
(page 21)

Warbler, Rufous-capped
Basileuterus rufifrons
(page 21)

Warbler, Mourning
Geothlypis philadelphia
(page 21)

Warbler, Swainson's
Limnothlypis swainsonii
(page 21)

Warbler, Nashville
Oreothlypis ruficapilla
(page 21)

Warbler, Tennessee
Oreothlypis peregrina
(page 21)

Warbler, Orange-crowned
Oreothlypis celata
(page 21)

Warbler, Townsend's
Setophaga townsendi
(page 21)

Warbler, Palm
Setophaga palmarum
(page 21)

Warbler, Virginia's
Oreothlypis virginiae
(page 21)

Warbler, Pine
Setophaga pinus
(page 21)

Warbler, Wilson's
Cardellina pusilla
(page 21)

Warbler, Prairie
Setophaga discolor
(page 21)

Warbler, Worm-eating
Helmitheros vermivorum
(page 21)

Warbler, Prothonotary
Protonotaria citrea
(page 21)

Warbler, Yellow
Setophaga petechia
(pages 10, 21)

Warbler, Red-faced
Cardellina rubrifrons
(page 21)

Warbler, Yellow-rumped
Setophaga coronata
(page 21)

Warbler, Yellow-throated
Setophaga dominica
(page 21)

 Whale, Long-finned Pilot
Globicephala melas
(page 78)

 Warblers, Assorted Wood
Parulidae
(page 44)

 Whale, North Atlantic Right
Eubalaena glacialis
(page 72)

 Wasp, Digger
Argogorytes mystaceus
(page 64)

 Whale, Strap-toothed
Mesoplodon layardii
(page 78)

 Wasp, Tarantula Hawk
Pepsis sp.
(page 54)

 White, Cabbage
Pieris brassicae
(page 56)

 Watersnake, Green
Nerodia cyclopion
(page 66)

 Witch, White
Thysania agrippina
(page 85)

 Waterthrush, Louisiana
Parkesia motacilla
(page 21)

 Wolf, Maned
Chrysocyon brachyurus
(page 80)

 Waterthrush, Northern
Parkesia noveboracensis
(page 21)

 Woodpecker, Acorn
Melanerpes formicivorus
(page 9)

 Whale, Blainville's Beaked
Mesoplodon densirostris
(page 78)

 Woodpecker, Downy
Picoides pubescens
(page 63)

Whale, Blue
Balaenoptera musculus
(page 85)

 Worm, Red Wriggler
Eisenia fetida
(page 70)

Wren, Carolina
Thryothorus ludovicianus
(page 10)

Xenacanthus
(page 83)

Yandusaurus
(page 83)

Yellowthroat, Common
Geothlypis trichas
(pages 9, 21)

Yellowthroat, Gray-crowned
Geothlypis poliocephala
(page 21)

Zalambdalestes
(page 83)

Photo by Adrianne Mathiowetz

Rosemary Mosco is a science writer and acclaimed cartoonist. When she's not drawing birds, she's out in the field doing some amateur nature photography and trying not to feed the mosquitoes.

www.birdandmoon.com